THE SPIRIT OF

DARTM

PETER WHITE

HALSGROVE

First published in Great Britain in 2007

British Library Cataloguing-in-Publication Data
A CIP record for this title is available from the British Library

ISBN 978 1 84114 616 4

HALSGROVE
Halsgrove House
Ryelands Industrial Estate
Bagley Road, Wellington
Somerset TA21 9PZ
Tel: 01823 653777
Fax: 01823 216796
email: sales@halsgrove.com
website: www.halsgrove.com

Printed and bound by D'Auria Industrie Grafiche Spa, Italy

Introduction

Dartmoor is a wild and wonderful landscape, beautiful but lonely. It offers space, freedom, relaxation, spiritual refreshment and a challenge to the adventurer. It is a friendly place when the sun shines, but can be unforgiving if the elements turn against you. It offers one of the best-preserved archaeological landscapes in Britain, and its habitats and wildlife are of international importance. For all of these reasons it is designated as a National Park – a recognition of its many special qualities and a safeguard against undesirable change.

Bowerman's Nose on Hayne Down

Peter White has walked on Dartmoor for thirty-five years and worked for the National Park Authority for twenty-five of those years. His intimate knowledge of the area is reflected in this collection of beautiful photographs portraying the landscape he loves.

May it inspire you to visit and explore an exceptional and unique corner of Britain.

Peter White

Shelstone Tor in the West Okement Valley

Opposite: *Burrator Reservoir from Leather Tor*

A lonely tree and a winter sky

*Ponies above the Dart valley. The Dartmoor pony is much
loved and is the National Park's symbol*

The Widecombe valley from Bell Tor, with the village sitting prettily in the field patterns

Opposite: *Bowerman's Nose and Easdon Down*

Childe's Tomb, overlooking Foxtor Mires. Legend has it that Childe the Hunter, lost in a snow storm, disembowelled his horse and sheltered in the carcass, but nevertheless died

Looking east from Sharp Tor on Spitchwick Common

Evening light on Rippon Tor, looking towards Hamel Down

Left: *Top Tor and Pil Tor from Rippon Tor. Foale's Arrishes on the hillside is an abandoned Iron Age field system*

Right: *Remains of farm buildings below Pil Tor*

Haytor Down in late summer. The friendly face of Dartmoor moorland

The River Lyd on Lydford High Down

Changeable weather over Brent Moor

*Opposite:
Tavy Cleave and Ger Tor on a frosty morning. This is perhaps the most dramatic moorland scenery on Dartmoor*

A dewpond on Haytor Down adds to the lonely feel of the moorland

The Walkham valley above Merrivale

Tor Royal Newtake at Whiteworks. The walls in the central Dartmoor newtakes march across the moorland for miles

Haytor Rocks are prominent from miles around and
are a grand viewpoint over South and East Devon

Widgery Cross on Brat Tor, near Lydford

The Dewerstone rises above the River Plym, and offers the best rock-climbing on Dartmoor

Bench Tor gives an airy perch over the Dart valley

Greator Rocks on Houndtor Down have an almost mountainous feel about them

*Hound Tor seen
from Honeybag Tor*

Vixen Tor, looking rather like a grumpy Indian chief

Great Staple Tor from Roos Tor

Sunset from Middle Staple Tor

A lone tree against the evening sky with Haytor in the distance

A thorn tree surviving above the Becka Brook valley

Evening sun lights up a horizontal thorn tree above Blackslade Mire

Left: Wistman's Wood. One of the three remaining ancient upland oak woods high on the moor – a jungle of stunted trees, hung with mosses and lichens

Right: Black-a-tor Copse. Another of the relict woodlands, with gnarled and twisted oaks sheltering a wonderful collection of ferns

Beeches above Prewley Moor, lit by the evening sun

*Beeches by
Meldon Reservoir*

Falls on the West Okement above Vellake Corner

The Dart, looking downstream from Holne Bridge

*Low water levels
at Burrator Reservoir*

Reflections in the lakes on the Becka Brook below Hound Tor

Opposite:
The great rock overhang reflected in Meldon Quarry pool

Burrator Reservoir from the old railway line on Yennadon Down

The sinuous shape of Meldon Reservoir, which penetrates Dartmoor's highest country

*Fernworthy Reservoir at
low-water level*

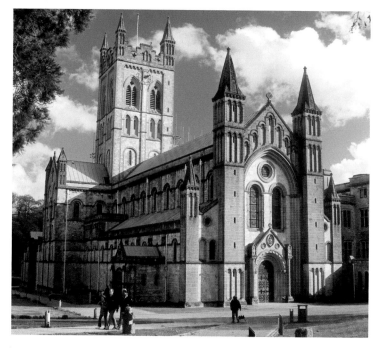

*Buckfast Abbey –
Dartmoor's most
popular visitor
attraction*

A prehistoric stone circle near Little Hound Tor

Windy Post on
Whitchurch Common,
marking an ancient
trackway across
the moor

Opposite:
Merrivale.
A wonderful collection
of Bronze Age hut circles,
stone rows and standing
stones, all right next to
the Princetown–Tavistock
road

*The stone circle at Scorhill,
near Gidleigh*

The engine house at Wheal Betsy mine near Mary Tavy, worked in the nineteenth century for lead, copper, silver and arsenic

Meldon Viaduct once carried the Southern Railway line over the West Okement valley, and now carries part of the National Cycle Network

*Nine Stones
at Belstone*

Haytor from near the old quarry

Look under the overhangs for an icy Aladdin's cave

Opposite: Sunrise and moonset at Hound Tor

A wonderful sky over Cosdon Beacon

On the Belstone Tor ridge

Haytor, dramatically framed

Opposite: *The lonely bowl of Taw Marsh, seen from Belstone Tor*

Looking down the Red-a-Ven Brook from West Mill Tor

High Willhays, Dartmoor's highest point

Haytor, plastered in snow, at dawn